Customer Service in Procurement Organizations

3 PRINCIPLES & 6 STEPS TO DRAMATICALLY IMPROVE CUSTOMER SERVICE

By Miguel Salcedo

Copyright © 2018 Miguel Salcedo
All rights reserved.

Content

Preface

Introduction

Problem Description

Customer service – A new definition

3 Principles to measure and improve Customer Service

Customer Service in Procurement Methodology (CSIPM^{SM}). 6 steps to measure and improve Customer service in procurement organizations

Customer Service Index model

Introducing and calculating CSIP^{SM} (Customer Service Index for Procurement organizations)

Customer Service Index for procurement organizations (CSIP^{SM}) formula:

Customer Service Index (CSIP) formula in excel format:

Customer Service Index (CSIP) calculation example:

Using Excel to calculate CSIP:

Customer service index improvement

Conclusion

About the Author

References

PREFACE

This book presents a new definition of customer service, introduces a new Key Process Indicator named "Customer Service Index for Procurement organizations (CSIP^{SM})", the formula to calculate CSIP^{SM}, and a new method named "Customer Service in Procurement Methodology (CSIPM^{SM}) to accurately measure, calculate and improve customer service in procurement organizations.

This methodology was developed after a thorough study of the procurement process and its impact on the success of a company. Procurement is such a critical process within a company's supply chain that its performance impacts directly the performance of a company.

In the early 1990s after being assigned to lead the Computer Systems support unit for the Procurement department, it was something of a shock to learn about the poor opinion internal customers had about the procurement organization. I was now a member of the underdog team and fell the necessity to turn that perception around, so I made it a personal challenge to discover and understand why this happened and in the end give a solution to the problem. At first I thought it would be a piece of cake to analyze and understand the problem, but it wasn't. The process is very complex and many factors come into play.

The book is intended first of all to benefit companies by dramatically improving the performance of the procurement process, and second, to vindicate procurement organizations and its personnel by significantly improving customer service through the implementation of the method and principles explained in this book.

In a coming book we will address customer service improvement for all kinds of businesses.

INTRODUCTION

Customer Service has been widely defined in business literature. Some authors have defined it as "An organization's ability to supply their customers' needs and wants" (1), "the process of ensuring customer satisfaction with a product or service." (2), or "the ability to provide a service or product in the way that it has been promised" (3). In a previous study, I had defined Customer Service in procurement organizations as "a Key Performance Indicator (KPI) that describes the general perception internal clients have about the Procurement department and the quality of its service" (4). However, in this book a new definition of customer service and a new way to measure and calculate this KPI are proposed, taking into consideration new elements recently discerned.

Unlike a commercial business serving the public where customer attention impacts customer growth and retention, in a procurement organization such element is not as decisive, because internal customers have in theory nowhere else to go to procure goods and services. Other elements besides customer attention impact customer service indicator significantly in Procurement organizations as they deal with internal company customers, impacting nothing less than production itself and therefore business performance. For this reason Customer Service indicator in a procurement process has that rare capacity to predict the potential success of the business as a whole. A poor measure of internal customer satisfaction means that the company is poorly prepared to supply the materials needed for production. In other words it could be said that No materials means No production, No sales, No money and No business.

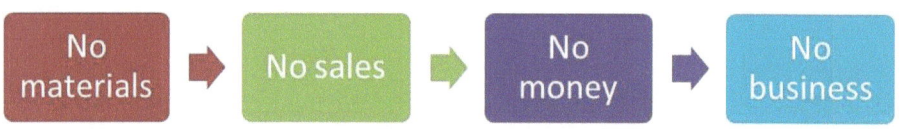

Figure 1 – No materials no business

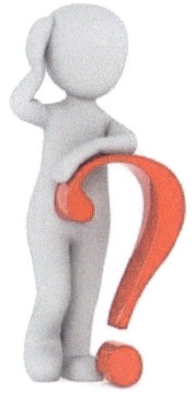

PROBLEM DESCRIPTION

Customer service in procurement organizations cannot be properly measured or improved simply by conducting customer satisfaction surveys alone. They are not enough. Although customer satisfaction surveys measure clients' perceptions about your service, they don't provide an exact picture of you service, nor do they show you what you need to do to improve your service. To improve your service the whole process needs to be looked into to determine which indicators have a direct influence on customer's perceptions. We have done that work and have determined those indicators that you need to measure and improve in order to impact customers' perceptions in a positive way.

Currently, customer satisfaction surveys are the only instruments used to measure customer service. In procurement organizations this approach produces inaccurate results because only part of the equation is calculated. At the same time, surveys are good to gauge body temperature but they don't provide the cure. With the new approach presented in this work not only customer satisfaction is measured but all other relevant elements that directly impact this indicator as well. A new formula and a method are presented to ensure that customer satisfaction surveys mark high the next time around. Before beginning to explain how to measure and calculate a customer service indicator in procurement organizations, a new definition of customer service is proposed as a result of this new vision:

CUSTOMER SERVICE – A NEW DEFINITION

A new definition of customer service is proposed by the author in this book taking into account new elements not previously considered. Thus,

Customer Service is defined as:

The perception customers have about the treatment and service received under expectations clearly set by the service provider.

The idea is very simple: If you treat your customers with courtesy and respect and at the same time you are able to deliver your procurement services within the promised time fame, your customer service indicator will be high. However, in order to make this a reality, internal clients besides being treated right, they also need to be informed about procurement processing times. If these two ingredients are in place, you are in the right path to customer service excellence.

As many of you know, achieving high grades in procurement customer service represents a real challenge because only about 50% of tasks (according to this author) are under the control of the procurement organization itself, the other 50% is under the control of suppliers. However, procurement departments do know suppliers' average delivery times even if they are currently not very good. This means that it is possible for procurement departments to get very close to excellent customer service if they do well the 50% that is under their control and at the same time inform their internal clients about suppliers expected delivery dates. In other words, if you provide great customer attention and give your internal clients an expected delivery date, you won't see your client complaining in your office unless that promised date isn't kept. It sounds very simple, however as it happens with everything else the obvious is often overlooked.

3 PRINCIPLES TO MEASURE AND IMPROVE CUSTOMER SERVICE

Customer service satisfaction like any other kind of satisfaction is closely related to the expectations people have about such service. Having this in mind, this new approach to measuring and improving customer service is based in three major principles:

1.Customer attention. This principle has to do with how good you treat your customers in terms of personal interactions.

2.Customer Expectations. Setting customer expectations straight first of all. Customer need to be informed about what to expect when they request our services. Expectations need to be known and pre-determined to standards that can be compared against.

3.Supplier Management. Making sure suppliers deliver on time as promised is a key principle.

Figure 2 – Principles to measure and improve Customer Service

CUSTOMER SERVICE IN PROCUREMENT METHODOLOGY (CSIPM^{SM}). 6 STEPS TO MEASURE AND IMPROVE CUSTOMER SERVICE IN PROCUREMENT ORGANIZATIONS

In order to measure customer service, we first need to determine what it is that customers want and what it is that they expect to receive from the procurement department.

Based on the study of the procurement process in large size procurement organizations (3), and according to the experience of the author, internal customers of procurement departments want and expect to obtain the following 6 determining factors:

- Courteous attention
- Fast treatment of purchase requests
- Information about Lead time / Expected Delivery date
- Information about Purchase request status
- Information about Purchase order status
- Compliance with lead time and expected delivery date

Figure 3 – What customers want and expect to obtain

STEP 1 COURTEOUS ATTENTION.

Courteous attention has to do with the way customers are addressed, responded and treated by procurement department personnel. In order to measure Courteous attention, a customer survey is necessary. Designate a person from the procurement department to design and execute this survey or request an expert to design it for you. The end result should provide with an indicator in the form of a number or factor expressed as a percentage of people who considered themselves satisfied with procurement attention. This will be a number from 0 to 100.

STEP 2 FAST TREATMENT OF PURCHASE REQUESTS.

Treatment of a purchase request does not refer to the actual purchasing time of the request. It has to do rather with how fast a buyer from the procurement department begins looking into a purchase request. Customers want their requests taken care of quickly, fast. How do you determine what is a reasonable Treatment Time?. The procurement department will arbitrarily set an average treatment time based on its Historic Average Processing Time and inform clients about it. This number is a percentage that indicates how many times the procurement department complies with the promise to treat purchase request within the established acceptable time frame.

STEP 3 INFORMATION ABOUT LEAD TIME / EXPECTED DELIVERY DATE

Here is where customer expectations begin to straighten out. Once a purchase request is finally looked into, analyzed or otherwise treated, you must inform your customers about how long they should expect to wait for their materials to be purchased and delivered to them. In order to maintain or improve customer service, Lead Time and Expected delivery time frame information needs to be calculated and timely informed to your customers. Lead Time and expected delivery dates can be obtained from procurement historic data.

STEP 4 INFORMATION ABOUT PURCHASE REQUEST STATUS

This is another piece of information that levels out customer expectations. The processing status of a purchase requisition indicates how far you are in the road to source materials for your customers. In SAP®'s Material Management (SAP-MM) system, a purchase requisition can be in any of the following three processing status codes (5): N (Not Edited), A (RFQ created - Request For Quote created) and B (Purchase order created). Not Edited means nothing has been done to that purchase requisition. RFQ created means the requisition has been treated, requests for quotes have been issued to suppliers and it's in the process to be purchased. And Purchase order created means the PO has been awarded to a supplier.

When the status of purchase requisitions is not informed to internal customers or if their request is in the N (Not edited) status code, your customer service grade is zero. The longer the delay, the worst your customer service grade will be. The goal is to minimize the Not Edited (N) status which is the essence of customer dissatisfaction along with poor status reporting. Assuring the treatment of all Purchase requests and informing clients with purchase requests processing status is the key to ensure positive customer service perception. The status information is obtained from a computer program that reports the status of each purchase request item. Once you have the status for each item requested, you send your customers an email or a text message informing them about the current status of their requisitions. The number calculated here is the percentage of times the procurement department effectively informs its customers about their purchase requisition status. Since this task can be automated to a great degree, the number obtained here should always be close to 100.

STEP 5 INFORMATION ABOUT PURCHASE ORDER STATUS

Again, to continue maintaining customer expectations at ease, this information must be sent out to customers. As it was mentioned above, In (SAP-MM) a purchase order is coded as a status B requisition. This means that a purchase order has been issued to suppliers and at this point it is necessary to inform internal customers that such purchase order has been issued. This can be accomplished by sending your users an email with all relevant information about their purchase order, including the expected deliver date. The procurement department should run daily or request the daily execution of the appropriate computer program that will obtain this information which will then be sent to each customer. The number calculated here is the percentage of times the procurement department effectively informs its customers about their purchase order status. Since this task can be automated to a great degree, the number obtained here should always be close to 100.

STEP 6 COMPLIANCE WITH LEAD TIME AND EXPECTED DELIVERY DATE

Finally, the procurement department will follow up with suppliers to make sure they deliver on time as promised. Daily, weekly or monthly reports can be run to determine how often our suppliers deliver as promised. This number is obtained by running a computer program that calculates the percentage of times a purchase ordered is delivered on time as promised by suppliers. Unfortunately this number is usually low. Designing and implementing a good supplier management program is a topic for a future article.

Figure 4 – Customer Service Index Model

INTRODUCING AND CALCULATING CSIP℠ (CUSTOMER SERVICE INDEX FOR PROCUREMENT ORGANIZATIONS)

This new index is designed and calculated according to the principles and methodology steps required to ensure excellent customer service as described above.

Let's define all variables involved and assign arbitrary weight values (*) to calculate customer service:

Variable	Variable ID	Weight
Courteous attention	CA	5
Fast treatment of purchase requests	FT	30
Information about Lead time / Expected Delivery date	EDD	5
Information about Purchase request status	PRS	5
Information about Purchase order status	POS	5
Compliance with lead time and expected delivery date	LT	50
Customer Service Index	CSIP	100

Figure 5 – Variables and assigned weights table

(*) these are weight values arbitrarily assigned to each variable. It reflects a percentage in the scale of relevance each variable has in determining a customer service indicator. In the opinion of the author these weight numbers represent a good rule of thumb based in his own experience. Each organization however, may assign its own weight numbers.

CUSTOMER SERVICE INDEX FOR PROCUREMENT ORGANIZATIONS (CSIP℠) FORMULA:

The formula to calculate a CSIP would be as follows:

$$\text{CSIP} = [(CA \times \text{weight}_{ca})/100 + (FT \times \text{weight}_{ft})/100 + (EDD \times \text{weight}_{edd})/100 + (PRS \times \text{weight}_{prs})/100 + (POS \times \text{weight}_{pos})/100 + (LT \times \text{weight}_{lt})/100]$$

Where subscripts $ca, ft, edd, prs, pos,$ and lt represent the weights assigned to their corresponding variable CA, FT, EDD, PRS, POS and LT.

$$CSIP = [(CA \times weight_{ca})/100) + (FT \times weight_{ft})/100)$$
$$+ (EDD \times weight_{edd})/100) + (PRS \times weight_{prs})/100)$$
$$+ (POS \times weight_{pos})/100) + (LT \times weight_{lt})/100)]$$

Figure 6 – Customer Service Index Formula

CUSTOMER SERVICE INDEX (CSIP) FORMULA IN EXCEL FORMAT:

The formula in excel format for CSIP would be:

=(((C3*D3/100) + (C4*D4/100) + (C5*D5/100) + (C6*D6/100) + (C7*D7/100) +(C8*D8/100))

Using excel's row-column notation C3, C4, C5, C6, C7 and C8 are equal to the values of CA, FT, EDD, PRS, POS, and LT variables respectively. D3, D4, D5, D6, D7, D8 are equal to the weight values assigned to each variable.

CUSTOMER SERVICE INDEX (CSIP) CALCULATION EXAMPLE:

1. Data

Let's assume that a procurement organization completed measuring each variable in a given period of time and the results were the following:

- Courteous attention (CA) = 60
- Fast treatment of purchase requests (FT) = 30
- Information about Lead time / Expected Delivery date (EDD) = 100
- Information about Purchase request status (PRS) = 100
- Information about Purchase order status (POS) = 100
- Compliance with lead time and expected delivery date (LT) = 30

2. Interpreting data

The above data is interpreted in the following manner:

For Courteous attention (CA) = 60, this procurement organization is declaring that 60% of its customers think the attention they get from the procurement department is courteous. Now, there could be various degrees of courteousness depending on how you design your survey. Therefore you decide what degree of courteousness will be considered acceptable. For example, If your survey sets degrees of courteousness 1 to 5 (low to high) then you could decide that for instance grades 1,2 and 3 are considered acceptable. In this case CA=60 means that 60% of customers surveyed graded you 1,2 or 3. If your survey only had 2 choices Yes or No for courteousness, then of course you would only consider YES answers in which case CA=60 means that 60% of customers surveyed voted YES. Please note that this is the only item that is calculated through a customer survey.

For Fast treatment of purchase requests (FT) = 30, this procurement organization is saying that 30% of its purchase requests were looked into, analyzed or otherwise taken out of the pending purchase request list, in a fast manner. "Fast" is a figure that your organization must define. Some organizations believe that treatment of purchase request within 28 days of their reception in the procurement department is acceptable. You decide what an acceptable number of days to treat a request is. The point is that this variable measures how often you treat purchase request within the acceptable time frame. The faster you start working in your customers' requests, the better your customer service grade will be. Customers resent when their requests aren't looked into fast enough. This number is calculated automatically by a computer program that reports the age of each purchase requisition not yet treated.

For Information about Lead time / Expected Delivery date (EDD) = 100, this procurement organization is saying that 100% of its customers received this information by email, text message or any other form, as soon as their purchase requests were looked into. This information should be given to your customers as soon as you receive a purchase request. When you do this, you are setting your customers' expectations to a more realistic time frame and therefore reducing the possibilities for future conflict with them. This information is calculated automatically by a computer program that obtains from the procurement system, lead time or expected deliver dates. Hopefully, if your procurement department sets up an automatic program and procedure to give out this information, this number should be always close to 100. If you do this manually, then it is possible that this number could fluctuate a lot.

For Information about Purchase request status (PRS) = 100, the procurement department is saying that 100% of its customers receive an update of their requisition status. Hopefully, if your procurement department sets up an automatic program and procedure to give out this information periodically, this number should be always close to 100. If you do this manually, then it is possible that this number could fluctuate a lot.

For Information about Purchase order status (POS) = 100, the procurement department is saying that once a purchase order is awarded to a supplier, 100% of its customers receive an update of their purchase orders. Hopefully, if your procurement department sets up an automatic program and procedure to give out this information periodically, this number should be always close to 100. If you do this manually, then it is possible that this number could fluctuate a lot.

For Compliance with lead time and expected delivery date (LT) = 30, the procurement department is indicating what percentage of items ordered, are delivered on time as promised by suppliers. This number is calculated by a program that calculates this indicator periodically, usually every month. As it has been mentioned above, this number unfortunately is usually low.

3. Calculating CSIP

Using the formula to calculate Customer Service Index (CSIP):

$$CSIP = [(CA \times weight_{ca})/100) + (FT \times weight_{ft})/100) + (EDD \times weight_{edd})/100) + (PRS \times weight_{prs})/100) + (POS \times weight_{pos})/100) + (LT \times weight_{lt})/100)]$$

Substituting values in formula:

$$CSIP = [(60*5/100) + (30*30/100) + (100*5/100) + (100*5/100) + (100*5/100) + (30*50/100)]$$

We get the following result: **CSIP = 42**

This would be the Customer Service Index for this particular procurement department for a particular period of time. It also means that customer service level is 42%. (from 1 to 100, where 100 is the highest mark)

USING EXCEL TO CALCULATE CSIP:

Given The formula in excel format for CSIP:

=((C3*D3/100) + (C4*D4/100) + (C5*D5/100) + (C6*D6/100) + (C7*D7/100) +(C8*D8/100))

Using excel's row-column notation C3, C4, C5, C6, C7 and C8 are equal to the values of CA, FT, EDD, PRS, POS, and LT variables respectively. D3, D4, D5, D6, D7, D8 are equal to the weight values assigned to each variable. The excel worksheet will look like this:

	A	B	C	D	E
					fx =((C3*D3/100) + (C4*D4/100) + (C5*D5/100) + (C6*D6/100) + (C7*D7/100) +(C8*D8/100))
1					
2	Variable	Variable ID	Value	Weight	Customer Service
3	Courteous attention	CA	60	5	3
4	Fast treatment of purchase requests	FT	30	30	9
5	Information about Lead time / Expected Delivery date	EDD	100	5	5
6	Information about Purchase request status	PRS	100	5	5
7	Information about Purchase order status	POS	100	5	5
8	Compliance with lead time and expected delivery date	LT	30	50	15
9	Customer Service Indicator	CSI	420	100	42
10					

Figure 7 – Customer Service Index - Excel calculation

CUSTOMER SERVICE INDEX IMPROVEMENT

The whole idea is to improve your numbers every time. Improving an index or indicator means taking the necessary actions to make that number better next time. Let's use the numbers in our example above to explain possible actions that can be taken to improve our index.

In the first month, we notice that the lowest scores were given for "Courteous attention = 60", "Fast treatment of purchase requests = 30" and "Compliance with lead time and expected delivery dates = 30)":

First Month measurement

Variable	Variable ID	Value	Weight	Customer Service Index
Courteous attention	CA	60	5	3
Fast treatment of purchase requests	FT	30	30	9
Compliance with lead time and expected delivery date	LT	30	50	15
Customer Service Index	CSIP	420	100	27

Figure 8 – Lowest scores table

Data Analysis:

- The above three variables add up to 27 points of our index and make up for 64.2% of overall CSIP (total of 42). Here we have a big opportunity for improvement
- These three variables make up for 85% of customer service weight. That is why our first month's measurement was so low (42). Remember Pareto?
- The first two low score variables: Courteous attention and Fast treatment of purchase requests, are variables fully controllable within the procurement organization
- The last low score variable: Compliance with lead time and expected delivery dates, is mostly out of the control of the procurement organization.

Possible Actions:

- Design and plan a training program to improve courtesy treatment by procurement staff
- Find out why procurement staff is not treating purchase requisitions on time
- Begin a Supplier management program to improve on time delivery.

This is just a small sample of data analysis and actions that can be taken to improve your Customer Service Index. Team work, data analysis and management involvement are some sure ingredients for success. If your procurement department works and measures CSIP every month, and take appropriate actions, your customer service index will show an ascending trend line, like in the following sample charts:

Customer Service in Procurement Organizations

Month	CSIP
Jan	42
Feb	47
Mar	52
Apr	57
May	62
Jun	67
Jul	72
Ago	77
Sep	82
Oct	87
Nov	92
Dec	97

Figure 9 – Customer Service index – sample data month by month

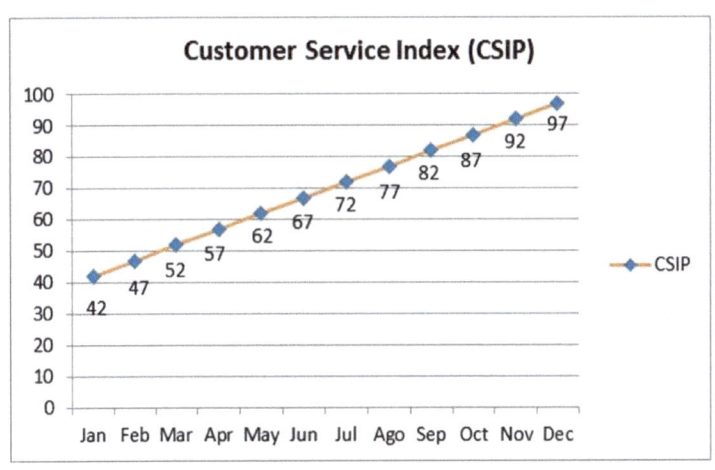

Figure 10 – Customer Service index ascending trend line chart

35

CONCLUSION

Customer Service is the perception customers have about the treatment and service received under expectations clearly set by the service provider. If customers are treated with courtesy and respect and procurement services are delivered within the promised time frame, your customer service indicator will be high. Customer service in procurement organizations cannot be measured simply by conducting customer satisfaction surveys among their users. Customer satisfaction surveys only measure clients' perceptions about your service. Other hard data facts and realities of the procurement process need to be measured such as procurement processing times, in order to properly calculate a customer service indicator. So far only customer satisfaction surveys are used to measure customer service. In procurement organizations this approach produces inaccurate results because only part of the equation is calculated. With the new approach presented in this work, an integral more complete and accurate Customer Service indicator can be calculated by including not just customer satisfaction data but all other relevant elements that comprise this Key performance indicator (KPI).

Courteous attention, Fast treatment of purchase requests, Information about Lead time / Expected Delivery date, Information about Purchase request status, Information about Purchase order status and Compliance with lead time and expected delivery dates, are the key elements used to calculate Customer Service Indicator (CSI). These elements are derived from principles of customer attention, customer expectations clearly established and Supply management programs. The formula to calculate CSI is presented and examples are shown to learn how to calculate this indicator.

ABOUT THE AUTHOR

Miguel Salcedo is a computer scientist graduated from Southern Illinois University. With more than 30 years of experience in Information Technology and procurement, he has helped companies achieve dramatic business process improvements through the use of computer technologies, quality management techniques and self-developed methodologies. He's been a speaker at international technology conferences and has published work in scientific journals.

His company Salcedo Consulting is a boutique procurement firm dedicated to providing procurement operations and strategy solutions, project management, business process improvement and data analysis. Through proprietary methodologies his firm has a program to improve the perception and value recognition of procurement departments.

Miguel currently lives in Orlando, Florida with his wife Carolina and their 4 children.

You may contact the author at his e-mail address: salcedoms@gmail.com or through his website www.miguelsalcedo.site . He is available for consultancy services, training workshops and speaking appearances both in English or Spanish.

REFERENCES

(1) Hanson, W (2000). Principles of Internet Marketing, Cincinnati, Ohio: South-Western

(2) Staff, I. (2015, May 16). Customer Service. Retrieved March 20, 2017, from http://www.investopedia.com/terms/c/customer-service.asp

(3) Rai, A. K. (2013). *Customer relationship management: Concepts and cases*. New Delhi: PHI Learning.

(4) Salcedo, Miguel, Methodology for Fast Processing of Purchase Requisitions, Elimination of Backlog and Improvement of Customer Service in Procurement Organizations (December 8, 2016). Available at SSRN: https://ssrn.com/abstract=2918601

(5) SAP ABAP Domain BANST (Processing status of purchase requisition) - SAP Datasheet - The Best Online SAP Object Repository. (n.d.). Retrieved December 14, 2016, from https://www.sapdatasheet.org/abap/doma/banst.html

(6) (SAP®) SAP and other SAP products and services mentioned herein as well as their respective logos are trademarks or registered trademarks of SAP SE (or an SAP affiliate company) in Germany and other countries.

Microsoft, Windows, Excel, Word, PowerPoint, and Project are registered trademarks of Microsoft Corporation in the United States and other countries.

All other product and service names mentioned are the trademarks of their respective companies.

www.ingramcontent.com/pod-product-compliance
Lightning Source LLC
Chambersburg PA
CBHW040332220526
45473CB00009B/2659